1 PIANO, 4 HANDS

PIANO DUET PLAY-ALONG
VOLUME 44

FROZEN

T0081320

To access audio visit:
www.halleonard.com/mylibrary

Enter Code
1899-9395-9521-7555

ISBN 978-1-4803-9197-0

Disney characters and artwork © Disney Enterprises, Inc.

Wonderland Music Company, Inc.

DISTRIBUTED BY

HAL•LEONARD®
CORPORATION
7777 W. BLUEMOUND RD. P.O. BOX 13819 MILWAUKEE, WI 53213

In Australia Contact:
Hal Leonard Australia Pty. Ltd.
4 Lentara Court
Cheltenham, Victoria, 3192 Australia
Email: ausadmin@halleonard.com.au

Visit Hal Leonard Online at
www.halleonard.com

CONTENTS

DO YOU WANT TO BUILD A SNOWMAN?

Music and Lyrics by KRISTEN ANDERSON-LOPEZ
and ROBERT LOPEZ

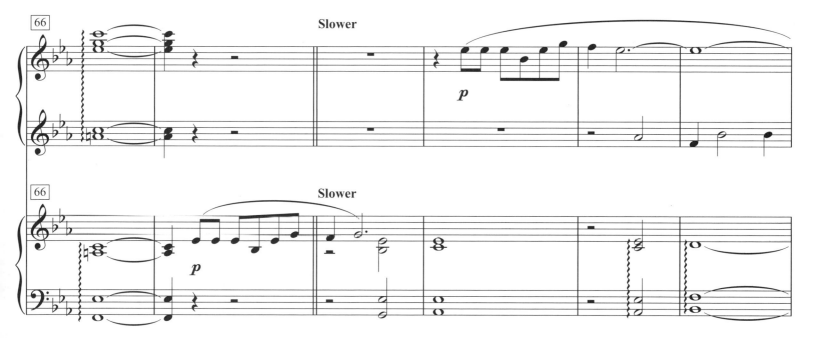

FOR THE FIRST TIME IN FOREVER

Music and Lyrics by KRISTEN ANDERSON-LOPEZ
and ROBERT LOPEZ

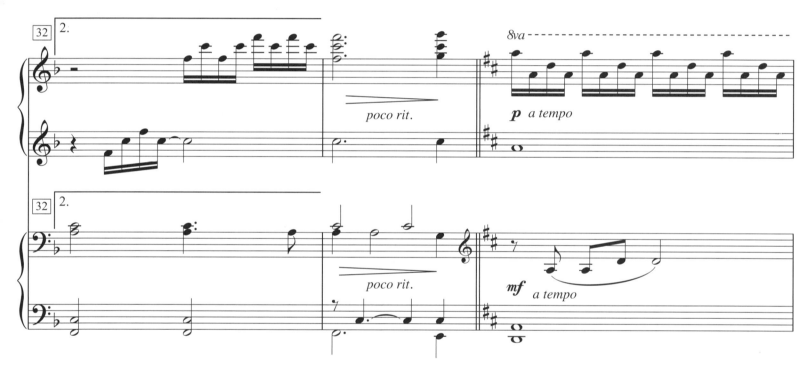

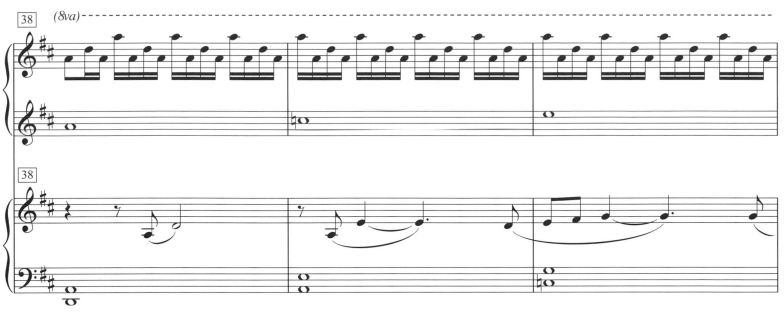

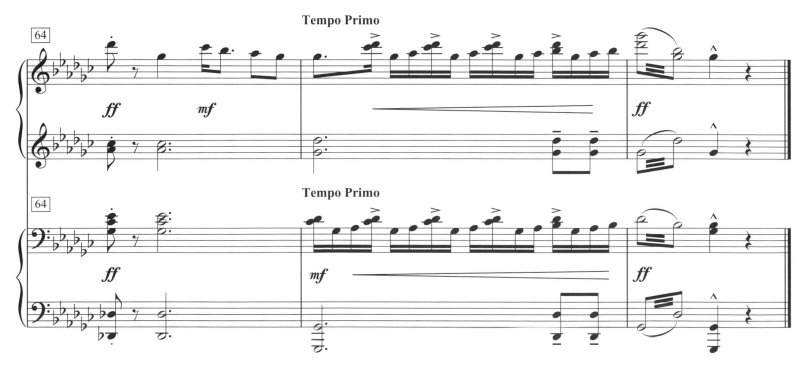

LOVE IS AN OPEN DOOR

Music and Lyrics by KRISTEN ANDERSON-LOPEZ
and ROBERT LOPEZ

LET IT GO

Music and Lyrics by KRISTEN ANDERSON-LOPEZ
and ROBERT LOPEZ

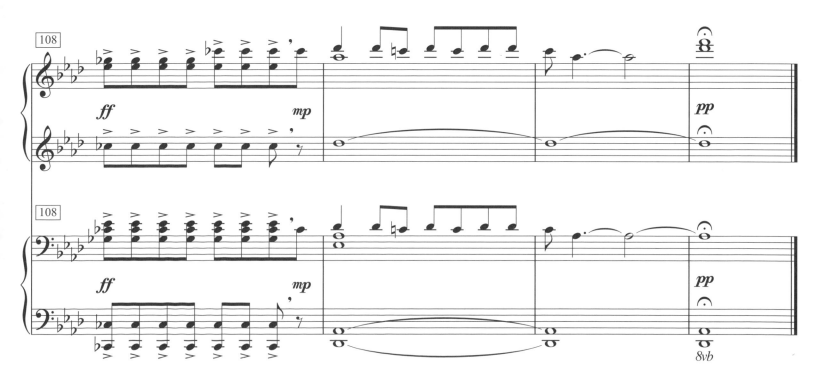

IN SUMMER

Music and Lyrics by KRISTEN ANDERSON-LOPEZ
and ROBERT LOPEZ

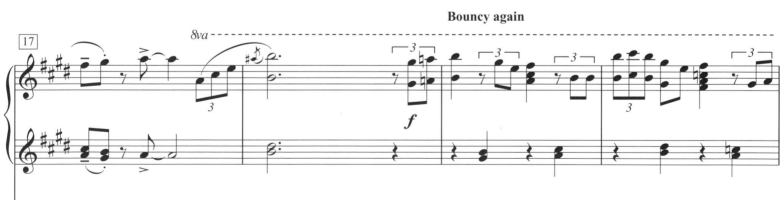

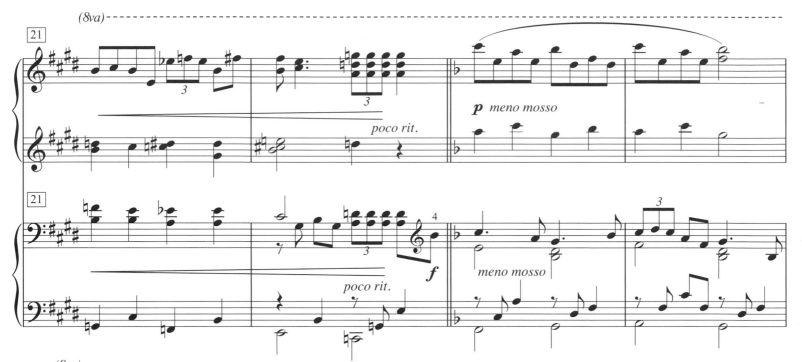

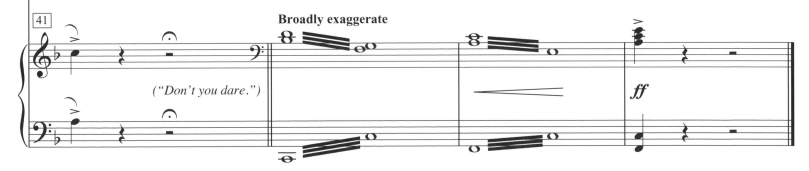

FIXER UPPER

Music and Lyrics by KRISTEN ANDERSON-LOPEZ
and ROBERT LOPEZ

REINDEER(S) ARE BETTER THAN PEOPLE

Music and Lyrics by KRISTEN ANDERSON-LOPEZ
and ROBERT LOPEZ

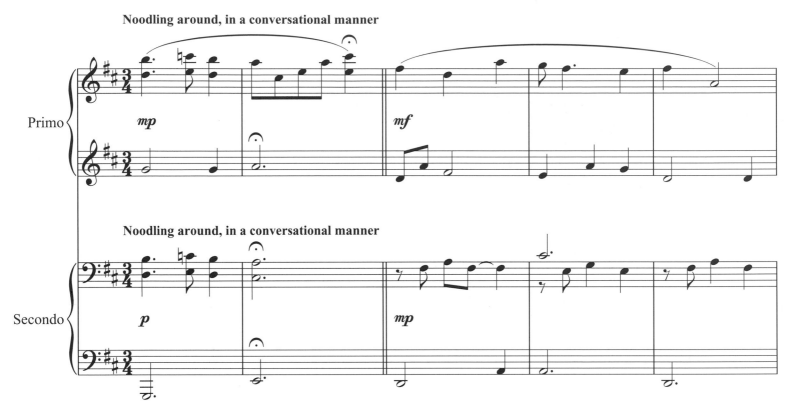

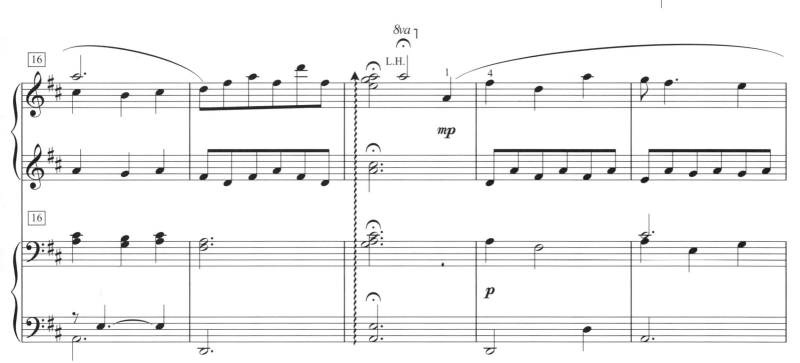

PIANO DUETS

The **Piano Duet Play-Along** series is an excellent source for 1 piano, 4 hand duets in every genre! It also gives you the flexibility to rehearse or perform piano duets anytime, anywhere! Play these delightful tunes with a partner, or use the accompanying audio to play along with either the Secondo or Primo part on your own. The audio files are enhanced so performers can adjust the recording to any tempo without changing pitch.

1. Piano Favorites
00290546 Book/CD Pack $14.95

2. Movie Favorites
00290547 Book/CD Pack $14.95

3. Broadway for Two
00290548 Book/CD Pack $14.95

4. The Music of Andrew Lloyd Webber™
00290549 Book/CD Pack $14.95

5. Disney Favorites
00290550 Book/CD Pack $14.95

6. Disney Songs
00290551 Book/CD Pack $14.95

7. Classical Music
00290552 Book/CD Pack $14.95

8. Christmas Classics
00290554 Book/CD Pack $14.95

9. Hymns
00290556 Book/CD Pack $14.95

10. The Sound of Music
00290557 Book/CD Pack $17.99

11. Disney Early Favorites
00290558 Book/CD Pack $16.95

12. Disney Movie Songs
00290559 Book/CD Pack $16.95

13. Movie Hits
00290560 Book/CD Pack $14.95

14. Les Misérables
00290561 Book/CD Pack $16.95

15. God Bless America® & Other Songs for a Better Nation
00290562 Book/CD Pack $14.99

16. Disney Classics
00290563 Book/CD Pack $16.95

19. Pirates of the Caribbean
00290566 Book/CD Pack $16.95

20. Wicked
00290567 Book/CD Pack $16.99

21. Peanuts®
00290568 Book/CD Pack $16.99

22. Rodgers & Hammerstein
00290569 Book/CD Pack $14.99

23. Cole Porter
00290570 Book/CD Pack $14.99

24. Christmas Carols
00290571 Book/CD Pack $14.95

25. Wedding Songs
00290572 Book/CD Pack $14.99

26. Love Songs
00290573 Book/CD Pack $14.99

27. Romantic Favorites
00290574 Book/CD Pack $14.99

28. Classical for Two
00290575 Book/CD Pack $14.99

29. Broadway Classics
00290576 Book/CD Pack $14.99

30. Jazz Standards
00290577 Book/CD Pack $14.99

31. Pride and Prejudice
00290578 Book/CD Pack $14.99

32. Sondheim for Two
00290579 Book/CD Pack $16.99

33. Twilight
00290580 Book/CD Pack $14.99

36. Holiday Favorites
00290583 Book/CD Pack $14.99

37. Christmas for Two
00290584 Book/CD Pack $14.99

38. Lennon & McCartney Favorites
00290585 Book/CD Pack $14.99

39. Lennon & McCartney Hits
00290586 Book/CD Pack $14.99

40. Classical Themes
00290588 Book/CD Pack $14.99

41. The Phantom of the Opera
00290589 Book/CD Pack $16.99

42. Glee
00290590 Book/CD Pack $16.99

43. A Merry Little Christmas
00102044 Book/CD Pack $14.99

44. Frozen
00128260 Book/Online Audio $14.99

45. Rhapsody in Blue
00125150 Book/Online Audio $14.99

FOR MORE INFORMATION, SEE YOUR LOCAL MUSIC DEALER,
OR WRITE TO:

HAL•LEONARD®
CORPORATION
7777 W. BLUEMOUND RD. P.O. BOX 13819 MILWAUKEE, WI 53213

View complete songlists at
Hal Leonard Online at **www.halleonard.com**

Disney characters and artwork are © Disney Enterprises, Inc.

0714